Bridget Jones: Mad About the Boy movie review

An In-Depth Analysis of Love, Loss, and Second Chances

Jimmie B. wald

Copyright page

Disclaimer page

This book is a Fan Unofficial Guide to Bridget Jones: Mad About the Boy, and was written independently for fans. It has no official affiliation, endorsement, or connection to Universal Pictures, Miramax, Working Title Films, Helen Fielding, or any other organization related to the Bridget Jones property.

The sole objective of this book is to provide information and amusement. The thoughts, interpretations, and analyses presented here are solely those of the author and do not represent the viewpoints of the production teams, actors, or creators of the Bridget Jones books or movies.

Although every attempt has been made to ensure the material supplied is accurate, the author does not guarantee that the content is reliable or complete. It is advised that readers independently confirm any information and develop their interpretations of the content.

The publisher and author disclaim all liability for any mistakes or omissions in this book, as well as for any results resulting from using its contents. By reading this book, you consent to absolve the publisher and author of any responsibility resulting from using the material.

We hope that this guide will help you better appreciate Bridget Jones: Mad About the Boy and Bridget Jones's lasting legacy.

Have fun while reading this book!

Table of content

Chapter one

The Fourth Diary: Examining "Mad About the Boy"

A pivotal point in the development of the adored romantic comedy series will be Bridget Jones: Mad About the Boy's 2025 debut. The fourth installment, which comes almost ten years after Bridget Jones's Baby (2016), comes at a time when Bridget Jones and her audience have grown up. Ever since Bridget first appeared on screen in Bridget Jones's Diary (2001), the society in which the film is situated has experienced significant social, cultural, and technical transformations. This chapter examines how the movie introduces Bridget's most recent journey while capturing the spirit of the mid-2020s and maintaining the charm and humor that made the series so popular throughout the world.

The eccentric, insecure thirtysomething who famously kept a diary in which she recorded her weight, cigarette consumption, and romantic mishaps is no longer Bridget Jones, who is now in her early 50s. Rather, she is a widowed single mother juggling her personal and professional lives while navigating the challenges of having two young children, Billy and Mabel. Following the death of her husband, Mark Darcy, who was killed on a humanitarian trip in Sudan, Bridget is getting ready to start dating again at the beginning of the movie. Compared to the previous movies, this premise instantly establishes a more solemn and introspective tone, indicating a change in the franchise's narrative focus.

Understanding Bridget's journey requires an understanding of the year 2025. With dating applications like Tinder playing a major part in her love adventures, the world has grown more digitally connected. The plot is pertinent to audiences today since it incorporates social media, streaming services, and the stresses of modern parenting. Bridget's technological difficulties, including her inability to access a streaming service, underscore the generational divide between her and her kids while also offering humorous moments.

Famous characters from the other films return in this one, such as Dr. Rawlings, who continues to give her scathing counsel, and Daniel Cleaver , who fills in as a confidant and babysitter. In recollections and flashbacks, Colin Firth's Mark Darcy makes an appearance, acting as a moving reminder of Bridget's past and the love she has lost. These recurring characters give the narrative continuity by keeping it rooted in the known while fostering the emergence of fresh dynamics.

Bridget's dual responsibilities as a mother and a professional woman are reflected in the film's urban and rural settings in London and the Lake District. The contrast between the peaceful countryside and the busy city life represents her inner conflict between clinging to the past and moving forward. Bridget's work as a TV producer and her kids' school activities are examples of contemporary landmarks and cultural allusions that keep the story grounded in the present while preserving the character's timeless appeal.

Breaking New Ground: The Differences in the Fourth Movie

With its daring deviation from the formula of its predecessors, Bridget Jones: Mad About the Boy stands out as a singular chapter in the series. The fourth installment goes deeper into themes of grief, resiliency, and self-discovery than the previous films, which concentrated on Bridget's romantic relationships and humorous accidents. This chapter looks at how the movie innovates both philosophically and narratively while maintaining the franchise's essence.

Mad About the Boy has a more mature and reflective tone, which is one of its most noticeable contrasts. The story's emotional center is Mark Darcy's passing, which compels Bridget to face her loss and rethink who she is as a widow and single mother. This change enables the movie to address themes of time passing, healing, and mortality in a way that appeals to older viewers. Though still there, the comedy is more muted and frequently tinged with melancholy, reflecting the intricacies of Bridget's new life.

With Bridget navigating the world of dating apps and age-gap relationships, the movie takes on the difficulties of contemporary dating head-on. As she struggles with social expectations and her vulnerabilities, her romance with Roxster, a younger man who approaches her on Tinder, offers both humorous and moving moments. This plotline offers a novel viewpoint on love and companionship while reflecting the changing attitudes about relationships and age differences in the 2020s.

Although romance is still a major theme, Bridget's relationships with her kids, friends, and extended family are given more attention in Mad About the Boy. The warmth and genuineness of her relationship with Billy and Mabel emphasize the pleasures and difficulties of being a single parent. The complexities of her "urban family," which consists of Tom, Jude, and Shazzer, who offer constant support and comedic relief, are also explored in the movie. These connections give the story more complexity and highlight Bridget's development as a person.

The franchise gains new vitality and diversity with the arrival of new characters like Isla Fisher's Rebecca and Chiwetel Ejiofor's Scott Wallaker. Rebecca, Bridget's new neighbor, brings a dash of humor and quirkiness, while Scott, a science teacher and single father, acts as Bridget's realistic and sympathetic opposite. The film's attractiveness and relevancy are increased by these people, who represent the inclusive and multicultural aspects of modern society.

The film stands out as a more sophisticated and genuine depiction of love and sorrow because of its subtle approach.

Chapter two

Production History

The process of making Bridget Jones: Mad About the Boy a reality was a protracted and complex one, filled with logistical difficulties, creative obstacles, and a strong dedication to respecting the franchise's past. This chapter explores how the project progressed from concept to reality as it dives into the film's development and pre-production phases.

Long before Mad About the Boy was formally announced in October 2022, the seeds were sown. The author of Bridget Jones, Helen Fielding, continued Bridget's journey as a bereaved single mother navigating contemporary life in her 2013 book of the same name. Readers were moved by the book's mature issues and sad tone, which sparked conversations about a possible movie adaptation. However, scheduling disputes, artistic disagreements, and the difficulties of translating a more introspective story for the screen caused delays in the project.

The idea of a fourth Bridget Jones movie had begun to take shape by 2020. The production studio that produced the earlier installments, Working Title Films, has shown interest in adapting Fielding's most recent book. To create a screenplay that struck a mix of heart, humor, and emotional depth, Fielding worked closely with screenwriters Abi Morgan and Dan Mazer. The team's goal was to produce a narrative that would appeal to both new viewers and devoted followers.

The project was directed by Michael Morris, who is well-known for his work on Leslie and Better Call Saul. Morris gave the franchise a new angle by focusing on a character-driven narrative and a more sophisticated take on humor. His idea for the movie was to examine Bridget's development as a person while tackling themes of self-discovery, resiliency, and bereavement. Morris collaborated extensively with Fielding and the screenwriters to make sure the script had modern features while staying faithful to the novels' spirit.

There were difficulties throughout the pre-production stage. Choosing how to respond to Mark Darcy's death, a major plot point in the book, was one of the biggest challenges. To preserve emotional resonance, the creative team decided to combine flashbacks and recollections, rather than limiting Mark's presence to just memories. Furthermore, careful preparation and organization were needed to manage the logistics of filming in several places, such as London and the Lake District.

With funding from Working Title Films and Miramax, the movie was expected to have a $60 million budget. The choice to release the movie on Peacock and in theaters in the US at the same time complicated the financial strategy even more. To guarantee a successful release, the production team collaborated closely with Universal Pictures, making use of the studio's extensive worldwide distribution network to expand the film's audience.

During pre-production, the cast and crew contributed to multiple changes to the screenplay. Bridget's character was greatly influenced by Renée Zellweger, who used her personal experiences and wisdom to give the part nuance and realism. Fielding's novel was captured in the final script, which also added new components to make the plot interesting and fresh while maintaining a careful balance between humor and pathos.

Casting Choices: New Faces and Returning Stars

Bridget Jones: Mad About the Boy's casting process was a meticulously planned attempt to strike a balance between tradition and creativity. It took careful planning to bring back cherished characters while adding new faces to maintain continuity and novelty. This chapter examines the casting choices that influenced the movie, emphasizing the reappearance of well-known actors and the inclusion of gifted up-and-coming actors.

Since Renée Zellweger's portrayal of Bridget Jones had come to represent the franchise, her return was inevitable. Zellweger's preparation, which included putting on weight to match Bridget's age and way of life, demonstrated her dedication to the part. To make Bridget's journey seem genuine and approachable, she also collaborated closely with the director and screenwriters. Zellweger's portrayal in Mad About the Boy was universally acclaimed for its comic timing and emotional depth, solidifying her position as the show's main character.

Another highlight of the movie was Hugh Grant's reenactment of the endearing but roguish Daniel Cleaver. Grant added much-needed humor and brightness to the part with his trademark charm and wit. The transformation of his role from a romantic interest to a helpful buddy gave the narrative a fresh perspective and demonstrated Grant's range as an actor.

Emma Thompson made a comeback as the witty and astute Dr. Rawlings, delivering her signature mix of wit and sagacity. The film's high point was the chemistry and banter between Zellweger and Thompson, which produced some of the most memorable scenes. Her persona's function as Bridget's confidante and mentor gave the story more emotional depth.

The story's emotional center was Colin Firth's character's death, therefore his return as Mark Darcy was bittersweet. Audiences were reminded of Bridget's lost love by Firth's moving and sincere depiction of Mark in flashbacks and memories. Despite his brief appearance, he had a vital role in the film's emotional impact.

Several new characters were introduced in the movie, and each one added a distinct personality and viewpoint to the narrative. As Scott Wallaker, a science teacher and single father who befriends Bridget, Chiwetel Ejiofor joins the cast. In contrast to Bridget's more erratic nature, Ejiofor's realistic and sympathetic performance gave the movie depth.

Roxster, portrayed by Leo Woodall, is a younger man who uses Tinder to approach Bridget. The plot of Woodall's character examined the difficulties of age-gap relationships, and his charm and charisma made Roxster a favorite among fans. Leila Farzad, Nico Parker, Josette Simon, and Isla Fisher completed the cast, each contributing special skills to the movie.

Bridget's children, Billy and Mabel, played important parts in the movie's success. Following a thorough search, Mila Jankovic and Casper Knopf were chosen to play Mabel and Billy, respectively. Their sequences are among the most moving in the movie because of their organic performances and chemistry with Zellweger, which infused the family dynamic with warmth and genuineness.

Filming at Sky Studios Elstree: Behind the Scenes

Filming for Bridget Jones: Mad About the Boy was a huge undertaking, involving locations in the Lake District and Sky Studios Elstree in London. From set design and cinematography to the difficulties of filming during a pandemic, this chapter offers an intimate look at the behind-the-scenes work that made the movie possible.

Mad About the Boy was primarily filmed at Sky Studios Elstree, a recently established facility in London. The production team found the ideal setting in the studio's expansive soundstages and state-of-the-art equipment to fully realize Bridget's universe. Because the studio was close to London, it was also simple to reach famous places like Bridget's flat and the TV studio where she works.

Art director Su Whitaker and production designer Mark Tildesley worked together to create the movie's set. Known for his work on

Paddington 2 and The Electrical Life of Louis Wain, Tildesley sought to create a world that was both visually rich and engrossing, reflecting Bridget's journey and personality. For instance, Bridget's apartment was furnished with unique accents and furnishings that expressed her personality, creating a homey and lived-in sense.

Another standout feature of the movie's design was the TV studio set, where Bridget works as a producer. The set was painstakingly designed to mimic a contemporary newsroom, complete with cutting-edge machinery and a flurry of activity. The situations felt more realistic and relevant because of the meticulous attention to detail.

Mad About the Boy benefited from the return of cinematographer Andrew Dunn, who had contributed to the earlier Bridget Jones movies. Dunn's use of warm hues and natural lighting produced an eye-catching look that went well with the film's poignant mood. The sequences in the Lake District, in particular, were filmed with an emphasis on the landscape's natural beauty, which stands in sharp contrast to London's modern settings.

The COVID-19 pandemic presented serious difficulties for the manufacturer, requiring frequent testing and stringent safety procedures. When not filming, the actors and staff wore masks and safety gear on set by social distancing norms. Notwithstanding these obstacles, the group stayed dedicated to producing a top-notch movie, and Morris and the producers put in countless hours to guarantee a seamless production.

Following three months of arduous effort, filming concluded on August 8, 2024. Reflecting on the difficulties and successes of the production, the cast and crew held a modest wrap party to commemorate the film's completion. The finished creation, which brought humor, emotion, and realism to Bridget Jones' most recent voyage, was a credit to their commitment and inventiveness.

Chapter three

The Creative Team

The movie filmmaker Michael Morris gave the cherished franchise a new and complex viewpoint. Morris, well known for his roles in To Leslie and Better Call Saul, was entrusted with striking a balance between exploring deeper, more mature subjects and maintaining the humor and charm of the earlier movies. This chapter examines Morris's artistic vision for the movie, his storytelling style, and how he overcame the difficulties of helming a sequel with such a storied past.

Character-driven storytelling was at the heart of Morris's Mad About the Boy idea. His goal was to examine Bridget's development as a person, emphasizing her fortitude and capacity to rediscover happiness and love in the wake of tragedy. Morris wanted to emphasize Bridget's journey as a single mother and her re-entry into the dating world, in contrast to the previous films that focused on her love follies. This change necessitated a more reflective and emotionally impactful approach, which Morris accomplished by focusing on Bridget's connections and inner conflicts.

Maintaining the franchise's distinctive humor while tackling the movie's more somber subjects was one of Morris's biggest challenges. To avoid the slapstick tone of the previous movies, he worked hard with the screenwriters to make sure that the humorous moments felt genuine. Morris's experience in television drama—specifically, Better Call Saul—influenced his ability to combine humor and emotional nuance, resulting in a tone that was both touching and enjoyable.

To create a visual aesthetic that mirrored Bridget's journey, Morris worked with cinematographer Andrew Dunn. With an emphasis on natural lighting and vivid colors, the movie had a cozy, welcoming look. Morris captured the characters' subtle emotional states using close-ups and intimate framing, especially in sequences with Bridget and her kids. The film's visual richness was enhanced by the contrast between the calm Lake District vistas and the busy urban environs of London, which represented Bridget's inner turmoil and development.

Morris worked with the cast in the same collaborative manner. He urged the players to improvise and contribute, especially Renée Zellweger, who was quite familiar with Bridget's role. The ensemble was able to give genuine and captivating performances because of Morris's ability to foster a creative and encouraging environment on site. The film's emotional resonance and humorous timing demonstrated his attention to detail and dedication to character development.

Mad About the Boy's identity as a mature and poignant addition to the genre was greatly influenced by Morris's concept. His collaborative approach to production and ability to strike a balance between humor and emotional depth made sure that the movie connected with both new and devoted viewers. In addition to paying tribute to Bridget Jones's legacy, Morris's direction gave the series a daring and significant new path.

The Writing Team: Morgan, Mazer, and Fielding

Helen Fielding, Dan Mazer, and Abi Morgan worked together to create the screenplay for Bridget Jones: Mad About the Boy. Each author contributed their special talents and viewpoints to the project, resulting in a script that was both inventive in its storyline and true to the original work. This chapter explores the writing process and how the three of them collaborated to create a script that struck a balance between heart, humor, and emotional depth.

The storyline of Bridget Jones was significantly shaped by Helen Fielding, the film's author. Her deep understanding of the characters and their setting made sure the screenplay stayed faithful to the novel's essence. Fielding's contributions were very important in expressing the story's emotional core and portraying Bridget's voice and humor. The success of the movie was largely due to her ability to add humor and genuineness to the narrative.

The screenplay was given the franchise's trademark humor by Dan Mazer, who had worked on the earlier Bridget Jones movies. Mazer's comedic experience, which included working with Sacha Baron Cohen, gave the writing a sardonic and sarcastic edge. Along with expanding the franchise's humor to represent the contemporary dating scene, he collaborated closely with Fielding to make sure the humorous moments were genuine to the characters.

Known for her work on The Iron Lady and Suffragette, Abi Morgan gave the screenplay a more dramatic and reflective tone. The film's themes of bereavement, resiliency, and self-discovery were explored in large part thanks to Morgan's skill at character-driven storytelling. She collaborated with Fielding and Mazer to create a script that was both enjoyable and thought-provoking by striking a balance between humor and emotional depth. The passages that dealt with Bridget's bond with her children and her experience as a single mother were especially notable for Morgan's contributions.

Fielding, Mazer, and Morgan worked closely together to polish the script during the very collaborative writing process. To keep the screenplay coherent and faithful to the movie's concept, they met frequently to talk about character arcs, plot points, and tone. The writing was full of humor, heart, and genuineness because of the three actors' ability to integrate their unique voices and points of view.

Converting Fielding's work, which had a more episodic and introspective structure, into a coherent film story was one of the writers' greatest obstacles. The plot had to be simplified and streamlined while maintaining its humor and emotional center. One important artistic move that gave the movie depth and resonance was the inclusion of flashbacks and memories of Mark Darcy. To make these aspects seem pertinent and real, the authors also had to negotiate the difficulties of contemporary dating and age-gap relationships.

Working Title Films and the Collaboration with Miramax

Working Title Films and Miramax, two formidable production firms with a track record of making critically acclaimed and financially successful movies, collaborated to produce Bridget Jones: Mad About the Boy. The relationship between the two studios, their contributions to the movie, and how their cooperation made the project a success are all covered in this chapter.

Tim Bevan and Eric Fellner formed Working Title Films, which has been responsible for some of the most cherished British movies of the last few decades, such as the earlier Bridget Jones films. The studio was the perfect fit for Mad About the Boy because of its dedication to crafting great stories and its ability to strike a balance between creative integrity and commercial appeal. Bevan and Fellner were heavily involved with the film's creation and production, making sure it both pushed the franchise into new areas and remained faithful to its heritage.

Mad About the Boy was co-financed and distributed by Miramax, a company renowned for its strategic alliances and award-winning films, in collaboration with Working Title. The movie's worldwide popularity was largely due to the studio's proficiency in distribution and marketing. The production crew was able to achieve their artistic vision without sacrificing quality thanks to Miramax's assistance and additional resources.

Working Title and Miramax had a smooth working relationship, with both companies collaborating extensively to make sure the movie was a success. Their united objective was to produce a movie that both paid tribute to Bridget Jones' legacy and appealed to modern viewers. A bigger budget was made possible by the collaboration, and this money was utilized to improve the film's production qualities, such as the set design, photography, and special effects.

A major contributor to Mad About the Boy's success was its marketing strategy. Using their combined experience, Working Title and Miramax developed a plan that catered to both new and devoted fans. To capitalize on its romantic undertones, the movie's premiere was scheduled for Valentine's Day. The smart decision to release the movie simultaneously on Peacock and in theaters in the US increased the film's accessibility and audience.

Working Title and Miramax's collaboration paid off, as Mad About the Boy had a great box office run and favorable reviews. The success of the movie demonstrated the studios' dedication to excellence and their flexibility in responding to the shifting demands of the motion picture business.

Chapter four

Character Analysis

Mad About the Boy, the fourth Bridget Jones book, represents a major change in Bridget's personality. Bridget is now a widow and single mother negotiating the difficulties of loss, parenthood, and contemporary dating; she is no longer the eternally unmarried, self-deprecating thirtysomething of the previous movies. This chapter examines how Bridget's development and metamorphosis are portrayed in the movie, emphasizing the themes of resiliency, self-discovery, and fresh starts.

When the movie begins, Bridget is getting ready to start dating again following the passing of her husband, Mark Darcy. His absence hangs over the narrative, acting as a source of emotional distress as well as a driving force behind Bridget's development. Bridget's widowhood is depicted delicately and nuancedly, illustrating the complexity of grieving. She is poignantly reminded of the love she has lost by flashbacks and recollections of Mark, which offer glimpses into their life together. Bridget's everyday challenges, like attending to her kids' needs and handling the well-intentioned but frequently invasive counsel of friends and relatives, are intermingled with these moments.

The portrayal of Bridget's sadness is one of ups and downs rather than a straight line. There are times when she feels depressed, such as when she hears an old voicemail from Mark or when she assists her kids in releasing balloons that contain notes addressed to their father. However, there are also humorous and lighthearted moments as Bridget deals with the difficulties of single parenthood and the awkwardness of contemporary dating. A defining feature of the movie is its harmony of tragedy and humor, which captures the depth of Bridget's emotional terrain.

Being a single mother is one of the most important facets of Bridget's development in

Mad About the Boy. Her bond with her kids, Billy and Mabel, is shown throughout the movie with love and genuineness. Every scene demonstrates Bridget's love for her kids, from the stories she tells to them before bed to her attempts to keep them safe from her hardships. The difficulties of being a single parent are, nevertheless, depicted in the movie without holding back. Bridget frequently feels overburdened by balancing the demands of her children, her social life, and her profession. Some of the most poignant and sympathetic scenes in the movie are her struggles to juggle these obligations.

At the heart of the film's emotional essence is the relationship between Bridget and her kids. Billy is withdrawn and finds it difficult to communicate his emotions since he is still dealing with the loss of his father. In contrast, Mabel is more gregarious and eager to try new things. Through her interactions with her kids, Bridget demonstrates her development as a person and her tenacity and resolve to give them a secure and caring home. Through Billy's plot, which ends with a heartfelt homage to his father at the school pageant, the movie also examines the effects of Mark's passing on the family.

Bridget's re-entry into the dating scene is entwined with her experience as a widow and single mother. The video captures the awkwardness and uncertainty of managing relationships in the internet era by depicting modern dating with a blend of humor and realism. Some of the most humorous parts of the movie come from Bridget's experiences with dating applications like Tinder as she struggles with the expectations of online dating and the generational divide.

One of the main plotlines revolves around her relationship with Roxster, a younger man who approaches her on Tinder. Even though their romance is playful and enjoyable at first, it also calls into question age-gap relationships and cultural expectations. Although Bridget's self-doubt and uncertainties are evident as she adjusts to this new dynamic, her courage, and openness to new experiences demonstrate her development as a person. In the end, she uses her relationship with Roxster as a springboard for her self-discovery, which helps her connect with Scott Wallaker on a deeper level.

Bridget's development throughout the movie is characterized by her capacity to face her anxieties and seize fresh chances. In addition to finding love, her path involves rediscovering who she is and where she fits in the world. A moving reminder of Bridget's tenacity and growth is provided by the film's ending, in which she finds love with Scott while paying tribute to Mark. Bridget's development as a widow and single mother demonstrates her capacity to face life's obstacles with grace, humor, and tenacity, which is evidence of her character's timeless appeal.

The Return of Daniel Cleaver: The Character Redemption Arc

One of the most anticipated elements of the movie is the reappearance of Hugh Grant's character, Daniel Cleaver. Daniel has long been a favorite among fans because of his charisma, wit, and roguish manner. His persona, however, changes dramatically in this episode, going from a romantic interest to a confidant and encouraging buddy. Daniel's redemption arc is examined in this chapter, along with how his character changes and adds to the emotional depth of the movie.

Given his track record of dishonest and self-serving actions, Daniel Cleaver's return is immediately viewed with suspicion. But the movie makes it clear right away that Daniel has changed. Daniel has evolved into a more thoughtful and mature figure, no longer the womanizing cad of the previous movies. Him and Bridget now have a true friendship that is characterized by respect and understanding for one another. Some of the most touching and funny scenes in the movie are from Daniel's work as a confidant and babysitter, which highlights his development as a person.

One of the main themes of Mad About the Boy is Daniel's journey of redemption. His transformation from a conceited bachelor to a more sympathetic and self-aware person is examined in the movie. His encounters with Bridget, especially the ones in which he gives her counsel and encouragement, emphasize this change. A crucial component of Daniel's character growth is his capacity to own up to his previous transgressions and make atonement, which gives his part more nuance and complexity.

Daniel's hospitalization following a heart scare is one of the most moving scenes in his redemption story. He is forced by this event to consider his life decisions and face his mortality. Daniel shares his apologies and his wish to come back in touch with his estranged kid in a sincere chat with Bridget. For Daniel, this vulnerable moment is a turning point that demonstrates his development and openness to change.

The film's high point is Daniel and Bridget's relationship, which offers a blend of humor and nuance. The same clever banter and chemistry that made them a popular couple in the previous movies continue to characterize their interactions. But their relationship has changed, and Daniel now takes on a more loving and encouraging role. Two important facets of their connection are his capacity to make Bridget laugh and his steadfast support of her quest for self-awareness.

Bridget's past and the decisions that have influenced her life are also brought to light by Daniel's appearance in the movie. His redemption narrative highlights the film's major themes of progress and self-discovery by drawing similarities to Bridget's journey. In the end, Daniel's development from a romantic interest to a helpful buddy is evidence of his character's enduring appeal and his capacity to change with the series.

Roxster and Scott Wallaker: The new characters

Bridget Jones: Mad About the Boy's introduction of new characters infuses the franchise with new vitality and viewpoints.

The characters of Roxster and Scott Wallaker, portrayed by Leo Woodall and Chiwetel Ejiofor, respectively, are essential to Bridget's romantic and self-discovery journey. The importance of these characters and how they affect the plot of the movie are examined in this chapter.

One of the franchise's most important new characters is Scott Wallaker, a science teacher and single parent. Chiwetel Ejiofor portrays Scott, as a sympathetic and realistic character who develops a close bond with Bridget. His employment at Bridget's kids' school offers a natural setting for their interactions, enabling their bond to grow naturally.

The more erratic and chaotic males in Bridget's life stand in stark contrast to Scott's persona. He is Bridget's perfect companion while she negotiates the difficulties of single parenthood and contemporary dating because of his cool-headed and considerate manner, which gives her a sense of security and stability. The film delicately and nuanced examines their connection, emphasizing the respect and understanding that grow between them.

The bond between Scott and Bridget's kids is among the most endearing features of his persona. His capacity to empathize with Billy and Mabel, especially at vulnerable times, gives his persona more nuance and emphasizes his function as a caring and encouraging leader. The fact that Bridget and Scott end up falling in love at the end of the movie is evidence of how strong their bond is and how fresh starts are possible.

Another important new character in the movie is Roxster, who is portrayed by Leo Woodall. Roxster, a younger man who uses Tinder to pursue Bridget, offers a humorous diversion from the film's more somber themes. Their humorous and impromptu connection perfectly captures the thrill and unpredictability of contemporary dating.

Bridget's self-discovery journey is sparked by Roxster's character, who pushes her to accept new experiences and leave her comfort zone.

Although their courtship is lighthearted and amusing at first, it also calls into question age-gap relationships and cultural expectations. Although Bridget's self-doubt and uncertainties are evident as she adjusts to this new dynamic, her willingness to take chances and seize new opportunities is evidence of her development as a person.

Roxster's ultimate goal throughout the movie is to assist Bridget in regaining her self-esteem and confidence. Even though their relationship is short-lived, it is a significant turning point in her path that would eventually lead to a closer and more meaningful bond with Scott.

The story of the movie gains nuance and complexity with the arrival of Scott and Roxster, opening up additional possibilities for examining Bridget's personality and connections. Their presence ensures that Mad About the Boy is a suitable addition to the Bridget Jones franchise by highlighting the film's primary themes of growth, resilience, and fresh beginnings.

Chapter five

Themes and Narrative Analysis

The concept of grieving and the process of moving on after loss is central to Bridget Jones: Mad About the Boy. The film's emotional core is around Bridget's experience as a widow, providing a moving examination of how sorrow affects relationships, identity, and the quest for happiness. This chapter explores how sorrow is portrayed in the movie, looking at how Bridget deals with her loss and finds the fortitude to welcome fresh starts.

Bridget is dealing with the loss of her husband, Mark Darcy, who was killed four years ago in Sudan while on a humanitarian assignment. Throughout the narrative, Bridget is constantly reminded of the life she has lost by Mark's departure. The movie presents sorrow as a complicated and multidimensional experience while handling it sensitively and steering clear of clichés. Bridget's sadness is not a straight line; it comes and goes, showing up as spontaneous tears, quiet moments of introspection, and even moments of laughter.

Focusing on the little, commonplace moments that make Bridget think of Mark is one of the most potent ways the movie depicts grief. These moments, whether it's hearing an old voicemail, remembering his voice singing to their kids, or finding his possessions lying around the house, capture the enduring presence of a loved one who is no longer with them but never forgotten. The impact of grieving on Bridget's relationships is also examined throughout the movie, especially with her kids, who are dealing with their loss in various ways.

Bridget's grieving process is significantly influenced by her memory. A bittersweet reminder of their shared love, Mark's flashbacks and dream sequences offer glimpses into their life together. These times are more than just sentimental; they help

Bridget deal with her feelings and accept her loss. Even as Bridget starts to move on, the film's use of memory is especially powerful in emphasizing the lasting influence of Mark's presence in her life.

Bridget and her kids release helium balloons with messages for Mark in one of the movie's most heartwarming scenes. This custom, which keeps coming up, represents Bridget's slow acceptance of her loss and her capacity for forgiveness. It serves as a moving reminder that finding a way to honor a loved one's memories while welcoming new opportunities does not equate to forgetting.

Bridget experiences both strength and tenderness during her grieving process. From the immense pain of attending a celebration of Mark's life to the difficulties of being a single parent, the movie does not hold back when illustrating her troubles. But it also shows how strong she is and how determined she is to start over. Bridget's resilience is demonstrated by her capacity to find humor in the middle of her suffering, whether it be through her self-deprecating thoughts or her inept dating attempts.

The value of support networks in coping with bereavement is also emphasized in the movie. Bridget receives vital support from her friends, family, and even Daniel Cleaver as she copes with her loss. Their support and empathy provide Bridget with a feeling of belonging and community, letting her know she is not traveling alone. The film's message about going on after loss revolves around this theme of support and connection.

Mad About the Boy is a tale about having the guts to welcome fresh starts. In addition to healing, Bridget's grieving process involves finding her identity and her potential for love and joy. The movie's ending, in which Bridget falls in love with Scott Wallaker while paying tribute to Mark, serves as a potent reminder that life goes on even in the wake of tragedy. Bridget's fortitude and the eternal strength of love are demonstrated by her capacity to move on despite carrying Mark's memories with her.

Family dynamics and parenthood

A major focus of Bridget Jones: Mad About the Boy is parenthood, providing an emotional examination of the pleasures and difficulties of being a single mother to children. A major component of the film's emotional depth is Bridget's relationship with her kids, Billy and Mabel, which emphasizes the intricacies of family dynamics and the effects of bereavement on a family. This chapter looks at how parenthood and the changing relationships in Bridget's family are portrayed in the movie.

One of the most important facets of Bridget's character in Mad About the Boy is her status as a single mother. She is shown in the movie as a devoted and loving parent, but she is also frequently overburdened by the responsibilities of parenthood. Bridget is a likable and approachable character because of the genuine and humorous portrayal of her battles to juggle her social life, profession, and her kids' demands.

The way the movie depicts the day-to-day difficulties of being a single parent is one of its strong points. The film depicts the hectic and frequently draining reality of raising children alone, from juggling nighttime routines to handling school functions and parenting conundrums. Some of the most heartwarming and funny parts of the movie come from Bridget's attempts to overcome these obstacles, frequently with the support of her friends and family.

Bridget's family dynamics are significantly impacted by Mark Darcy's passing, especially her children. Billy is withdrawn and finds it difficult to communicate his feelings because he is still dealing with the loss of his father. In contrast, Mabel is more gregarious and eager to try new things. The movie highlights the various ways loss may impact a family by examining how each youngster copes with sorrow uniquely.

The bond between Bridget and Billy is especially moving. From urging him to compete in the school pageant to having emotional discussions about his father, the movie shows her attempts to establish a connection with him and assist him in overcoming his sadness. In addition to capturing the intense love and understanding that underlies their connection, these moments also highlight the difficulties of raising a bereaved child.

The value of friends and extended family in helping Bridget and her kids is also emphasized in the movie. Dr. Rawlings, Bridget's mother Pamela, Daniel Cleaver, and other characters are essential in offering both practical and emotional support. Their presence emphasizes how crucial connections and community are to overcoming the difficulties of being a single parent.

The film's portrayal of Bridget's "urban family," a close-knit group of pals who offer steadfast support and companionship, is among its most poignant elements. From providing child care assistance to giving guidance and support, their engagement in

Bridget's life highlights the concept of a chosen family and the value of establishing a support system.

The movie highlights the pleasures of childrearing while also acknowledging the difficulties of being a single parent. Every moment demonstrates Bridget's affection for Billy and Mabel, from the stories she reads to them before bed to her attempts to provide them with a sense of security and stability. In the end, the movie's depiction of motherhood is one of resiliency and hope, emphasizing how kids can make life happier and more meaningful even when they experience loss.

The film's ending, in which Bridget and her kids discover harmony and kinship, is proof of the eternal strength of family. In addition to conquering obstacles, Bridget's path as a single mother involves rediscovering the love and joy that accompany parenthood.

Middle-aged Modern Dating

The movie examination of contemporary middle-aged dating is among its most captivating features. Bridget's return to dating following Mark Darcy's passing offers a poignant and amusing look at the difficulties and possibilities of discovering love later in life. This chapter looks at how the movie depicts contemporary dating, including the intricacies of age-gap relationships and the usage of dating apps.

The discomfort and unpredictability of contemporary dating are depicted in the movie, especially through Bridget's experiences with dating apps like Tinder. Some of the funniest parts of the movie come from her attempts to figure out the internet dating scene, from creating the ideal profile to figuring out the frequently perplexing realm of online communication. The movie's realistic and hilarious depiction of dating apps emphasizes the generational divide and the difficulties of forming deep connections in the digital age.

One of the main plotlines of the movie is Bridget's connection with Roxster, a younger man she meets on Tinder. At first, their courtship is playful and enjoyable, but it also calls into question age-gap relationships and cultural expectations. From the disparities in life experiences to the criticism and scrutiny that can accompany such relationships, the movie examines the difficulties of dating someone much younger.

The movie also explores the particular difficulties of dating in middle age. As she navigates the dating scene, Bridget's doubts and self-doubt are evident; she worries about how she looks and wonders if she's ready for a new relationship. The movie portrays the dating experience in a way that is sympathetic and relevant while capturing the bravery and vulnerability required to put oneself out there following a loss.

The film's ability to depict dating in a way that strikes a balance between humor and emotional depth is one of its strong points.

Although Bridget's embarrassing interactions and mishaps provide many amusing moments, they also highlight the emotional costs associated with falling in love later in life. The movie's examination of middle-aged dating is one of resiliency and hope, emphasizing that pleasure and connection may be found at any age.

Mad About the Boy is a tale about discovering connection and love amidst life's obstacles. Finding a spouse is only one aspect of Bridget's dating journey; she also hopes to rediscover who she is and her capacity for love. The movie's ending, in which Bridget falls in love with Scott Wallaker, is proof of the enduring power of love and the potential for fresh starts.

The movie captures the intricacies and delights of discovering love later in life with its hilarious and poignant depiction of contemporary dating in middle age. Even amid loss and uncertainty, Bridget's path serves as a reminder that it is never too late to seize new chances and discover happiness.

Chapter six

Visual Style and Cinematography

The London locations of Bridget Jones: Mad About the Boy are crucial to the film's visual identity, acting as both a setting and a character. The city's dynamic energy, well-known sites, and varied neighborhoods create a rich tapestry for Bridget's voyage that reflects both the story's themes and her emotional state. This chapter examines how the film's narrative and emotional impact are influenced by its London locales and aesthetics.

The Bridget Jones series has always included London, and Mad About the Boy carries on this tradition. Because of the city's busy streets, welcoming bars, and lovely parks, the story is anchored in a setting that is both familiar and relatable. From the majesty of its ancient sites to the allure of its more subdued, private areas, the movie perfectly conveys the spirit of London.

Reflecting on Bridget's emotional journey is one of the most remarkable features of the movie's depiction of London. The busy metropolitan environments, including Bridget's flat and the streets of Notting Hill, represent her hectic and frequently stressful life as a single mother. On the other hand, Bridget's inner development and recovery are reflected in the tranquil surroundings of the Lake District, where she and her kids embark on a school excursion.

Several famous London locales that have come to be associated with the Bridget Jones series are included in the movie. With its eccentric furnishings and homey ambiance, Bridget's flat continues to be a key location, providing insight into both her character and motherhood. To establish a feeling of continuity with the other movies, the movie also returns to well-known locations, like the neighborhood bar and the TV studio where Bridget works.

New settings, such as the contemporary newsroom where Bridget conducts a live interview, give the movie a more current feel while also illustrating how Bridget's profession is developing and the times are changing. In addition to improving the film's aesthetic appeal, the utilization of these locations supports its themes of development and adaptation.

Warm and inviting color schemes, with an emphasis on natural lighting and vivid tones, define the film's visual aesthetics. In Mad About the Boy, cinematographer Andrew Dunn, who worked on the earlier Bridget Jones movies, creates a universe that is visually stunning and captivating. Intimate framing and close-ups are used to convey the characters' subtle emotional states, especially in moments with Bridget and her kids.

One of the main components of the movie's visual identity is the contrast between the urban and rural environments. The vibrant colors and dramatic compositions of the busy city landscapes capture Bridget's hectic and frequently exhausting life. The tranquil surroundings of the Lake District, on the other hand, with their subdued hues and gentle lighting, evoke a feeling of peace and introspection that reflects Bridget's inner development and recovery.

Symbolism and metaphor are also used in the film's visual aesthetics to strengthen its story. As a reminder of Mark's ongoing influence on Bridget's life, the white owl, which Mabel says goodnight to every night, is a recurrent motif that represents optimism and connection. Bridget's path of self-discovery and development is highlighted by the usage of mirrors and reflections in significant sequences.

New beginnings and the potential for happiness are symbolized by the film's ending, in which Bridget and her family celebrate New Year's Eve in a lively and joyous atmosphere. This scene's use of color and light evokes a feeling of coziness and hope, which supports the film's theme of resilience and optimism.

Character Expression and Costume Design

The costume design is essential because it acts as a visual language that conveys narrative ideas, character attributes, and emotional states. Steven Noble's outfits for the movie show Bridget's development as a person, from her eccentric and self-conscious look to her more assured and refined look. This chapter examines how costume design improves the film's narrative and aids in character expression.

A defining feature of Bridget's personality has always been her attire, and Mad About the Boy carries on this tradition. Her distinctive look, which combines comfortable, functional attire with oddball, mismatched items, captures her individuality and her experiences as a single mother. From her vibrant cardigans and patterned dresses to her functional yet fashionable coats and boots, the movie's outfits perfectly convey Bridget's distinct sense of style.

The way Bridget's outfit changes during the movie is among its most striking features. Her style becomes more sophisticated and self-assured as she works through the difficulties of modern dating, fatherhood, and sorrow, reflecting her development as a person. Her costumes' use of color and texture furthers her metamorphosis, with more structured forms and vibrant hues signifying her growing confidence.

The characters' personalities and emotional states are highlighted through the clothing throughout the movie, which also functions as a vehicle for character expression. For instance, Daniel Cleaver's roguish charm and growing maturity are reflected in his clothing. His transition from a conceited bachelor to a more sympathetic and self-aware person is highlighted by his fitted suits and relaxed yet fashionable attire.

The modest elegance and simplicity of Scott Wallaker's clothes capture his sympathetic and grounded personality. He is the perfect match for Bridget's more eclectic style because of his timeless silhouettes and muted colors, which convey stability and dependability. In stark contrast to the more mature characters, Roxster's youthful and fashionable outfit accentuates his impulsive and carefree nature.

To improve the tale, the movie's clothing also uses narrative elements and symbolism. For instance, character arcs and emotional states can be effectively communicated through the use of color. The softer, more subdued tones in the early scenes represent Bridget's loss and doubt, while her brighter, more colorful attire in the later portions of the movie represents her developing self-assurance and sense of self.

The costumes also feature the white owl, which is a recurrent motif in Mabel's nightly ritual. For instance, Bridget's owl-print pajamas reinforce the film's emotional core by acting as a visual reminder of the ideas of hope and connection.

From the thoughtfully selected accessories to the minor adjustments to Bridget's hair and makeup, the movie's costume design is distinguished by its meticulous attention to detail. By adding a sense of realism and relatability, these elements strengthen the characters' and their world's authenticity. The film's depiction of single parenthood is enhanced by the use of functional and practical attire, especially in sequences involving Bridget's kids. This emphasizes the joys and daily struggles of childrearing.

Analysis of Music and Soundtracks

The soundtrack and music are essential to heightening the film's emotional resonance and narrative themes. Craig Armstrong's score and the film's well-chosen soundtrack produce a rich aural environment that enhances the visual narrative. This chapter examines how the soundtrack and music enhance the film's thematic resonance and emotional depth.

A significant component of the film's emotional environment is Craig Armstrong's score, which offers a melodic setting that highlights the themes of loss, resiliency, and fresh starts. The film's emotional resonance is increased by the score's use of melodic motifs and orchestral arrangements, which evoke a feeling of coziness and closeness.

The score's capacity to capture Bridget's emotional journey is among its most noteworthy features. While the more upbeat and dynamic songs in the later portions of the film indicate her development and metamorphosis, the choice of softer, more contemplative melodies in the earlier scenes conveys her loss and confusion. Armstrong's skill as a composer is demonstrated by the score's ability to strike a balance between humor and melancholy, producing a musical narrative that enhances the film's narrative.

The soundtrack of the movie is a blend of modern and vintage tunes that capture the spirit of the period and Bridget's development. By using well-known songs from the earlier Bridget Jones movies, like "All by Myself" and "It's Raining Men," Mad About the Boy establishes a feeling of continuity and nostalgia with its forerunners.

Modern pop and indie songs, among other new additions to the soundtrack, give the movie a current feel while also mirroring Bridget's world's evolving terrain. The emotional effect of the story is increased by the inclusion of these songs in significant sequences, ranging from the humorous and lighthearted to the more somber and introspective ones.

The soundtrack of the movie also highlights significant plot points and themes, acting as a narrative device. For instance, Billy's rendition of "I'd Do Anything" at the school pageant serves as a potent reminder of Mark's ongoing influence on Bridget's life, evoking a poignant and intimate moment. The incorporation of this song, which has come to represent the Bridget Jones series, serves to further emphasize the film's themes of loss and love.

The film's upbeat and joyous music, which represents fresh starts and the potential for happiness, is played during the film's climactic New Year's Eve celebration. This scene's usage of music reinforces the film's message of resiliency and hope by evoking feelings of warmth and optimism.

The soundtrack and music of the movie are essential to heightening its emotional impact since they produce a rich aural environment that goes well with the visual narrative. Together with the thoughtfully chosen soundtrack, the score's ability to strike a balance between humor and melancholy produces a musical narrative that connects with viewers and strengthens the film's themes of loss, resiliency, and fresh starts.

Chapter seven

Cultural Impact and Reception

A flurry of reviews greeted Bridget Jones: Mad About the Boy's 2025 release, praising its humor, emotional depth, and development of the cherished franchise. The film's ability to strike a balance between the series' trademark charm and humor and the melancholy tone of Helen Fielding's book won accolades from critics. This chapter explores the film's critical reception, examining the themes, performances, and narrative decisions that both critics and viewers found compelling.

The return of Renée Zellweger as Bridget Jones was widely praised by critics, who praised her for giving the role nuance and realism. It was said that her portrayal of Bridget as a widowed single mother negotiating loss, parenthood, and contemporary dating was both moving and realistic. From Bridget's vulnerable moments to her humor and resiliency, Zellweger's acting encapsulated the subtleties of her emotional journey. Her reputation as the franchise's heart and soul was cemented when critics praised her for her ability to strike a balance between comedy and drama, highlighting her acting prowess.

Mad About the Boy's examination of sorrow and resiliency was one of its most lauded features. The film's delicate depiction of Bridget's loss journey, emphasizing the little, commonplace moments that encapsulated the complexities of grief, was well received by critics. Bridget was poignantly reminded of the love she had lost through the use of flashbacks and recollections of Mark Darcy, which had an emotional impact. A recurrent theme in reviews was the movie's ability to strike a delicate balance between heartbreak and hope, with humor and emotional depth.

Another compliment was the movie's courage to experiment and tackle novel subjects. Mad About the Boy, according to critics, marked a major shift for the franchise, departing from the romantic comedy template of the previous movies and entering a more sophisticated and reflective realm. The series' examination of contemporary dating, age-gap relationships, and single parenthood was viewed as a welcome and topical update that reflected the times and the shifting expectations of viewers.

Despite the film's mostly favorable reviews, some reviewers pointed out that the pacing was erratic, especially in the second act. Although it was funny, some critics felt that the Roxster plotline was underdeveloped and should have been given more attention. The choice to murder Mark Darcy also caused controversy among viewers, with some applauding the audacious narrative decision and others lamenting the passing of a cherished character.

The general view was that Mad About the Boy was a worthy addition to the Bridget Jones franchise, notwithstanding these complaints. The film's emotional depth, powerful performances, and ability to strike a balance between humor and heart won accolades from critics. The film's examination of loss, resiliency, and fresh starts struck a chord with viewers, guaranteeing that it would be regarded as a noteworthy addition to the series.

With a great box office performance and impressive streaming figures, Bridget Jones: Mad About the Boy was a commercial triumph when it was released in 2025. A calculated decision that optimized the film's accessibility and reach by releasing it simultaneously in theaters and on Peacock in the US appealed to both traditional moviegoers and streaming viewers. This chapter looks at the movie's performance at the box office, its success on streaming services, and the elements that made it so popular with consumers.

The movie made almost £10 million in its first weekend at the UK box office, where it opened at number one. Its Valentine's Day release, which capitalized on the love themes and drew in couples and franchise aficionados, was a major contributor to its popularity. The movie did just as well in other foreign markets, with especially high showings in Europe and Australia. One of the highest-grossing romantic comedies of the year, Mad About the Boy made over $150 million worldwide by the end of its theatrical run.

A calculated risk that paid off, the movie's simultaneous premiere on Peacock in the US drew a sizable viewership and created discussion on social media. The ease of streaming made it possible for the movie to be seen by more people, especially younger audiences who might not have seen the previous movies. The film's durability was also aided by its availability on Peacock, which had high attendance in the weeks after its premiere.

The movie's commercial success was influenced by several variables. Much excitement and anticipation were created by the return of Emma Thompson, Hugh Grant, and Renée Zellweger as well as the arrival of fresh talent like Leo Woodall and Chiwetel Ejiofor. Audiences responded well to the film's marketing campaign, which highlighted its humor and emotional depth, and its Valentine's Day release made the most of the romantic themes.

Another important element in the movie's popularity was its ability to strike a balance between innovation and nostalgia. Mad About the Boy attracted both new audiences and devoted fans by re-examining well-known characters and settings while experimenting with fresh ideas and plots. The film's examination of age-gap relationships, modern dating, and single parenthood was viewed as timely and pertinent, reflecting the shifting times and audience expectations.

Cultural Discussions Initiated by the Movie

Bridget Jones: Mad About the Boy provoked a variety of cultural themes, ranging from arguments about age-gap relationships and modern dating to discussions about bereavement and resiliency. The film's examination of these subjects struck a chord with viewers, inspiring contemplation on love, grief, and the difficulties of adjusting to life's changes. This chapter looks at the movie's cultural influence and the discussions it generated.

The film's depiction of loss and resiliency was one of the most important cultural discussions it inspired. Audiences found resonance in Bridget's story of reconstructing her life after losing her spouse and overcoming grief, which sparked conversations about the value of support networks and the intricacies of grieving. Many viewers shared their own stories of loss and healing, and the film's poignant depiction of Bridget's emotional journey was lauded for being genuine and relatable.

Intriguing discussions were also generated by the movie's examination of contemporary dating and age-gap relationships. Questions concerning social norms and the difficulties of dating in middle age were brought up by Bridget's connection with Roxster, a younger man she meets on Tinder. The way these issues were portrayed in the movie was regarded as both hilarious and thought-provoking, inspiring viewers to consider how relationships are evolving and how important it is to seize new opportunities.

Another important subject of conversation was how the movie portrayed family dynamics and single parenthood. Reflections on the difficulties and rewards of raising children alone were prompted by Bridget's struggles to strike a balance between her social life, profession, and her kids' demands. Many viewers shared their own experiences of being a single parent, and the film's emphasis on the value of community and support networks was hailed for being genuine and relatable.

The character development of Bridget Jones in the movie also provoked discussions about culture. Bridget's transformation from a self-conscious thirty something to a strong and resilient single mother was viewed as a potent and uplifting story that reflected the shifting social norms around women. The film's examination of Bridget's development and self-discovery struck a chord with viewers, inspiring contemplation on the value of accepting change and drawing strength from vulnerability.

The film's lasting influence and importance were highlighted by the cultural discussions Mad About the Boy provoked. Through examining themes of loss, resiliency, and fresh starts, the movie struck a deep and intimate chord with viewers, inspiring contemplation on love, loss, and the difficulties of adjusting to life's changes. The film's ability to strike a mix of humor and emotional depth made it a memorable addition to the Bridget Jones franchise, igniting discussions long after it came out.

Chapter eight

Comparisons and Connections

Each is more than 20-year-old Bridget Jones series and depicts a different stage of Bridget's life. Bridget's development from her early years as a self-conscious singleton to her experience as a widowed single mother is evidence of her character's timeless appeal. This chapter examines Bridget's development and transformation throughout the four movies, emphasizing the themes and narrative decisions that have shaped her path.

In the first movie, Bridget Jones's Diary, viewers are introduced to Bridget as a thirty-two-year-old unmarried woman juggling the demands of self-acceptance, profession, and love. She became instantly famous due to her humorous self-loathing, relatable fears, and charming awkwardness. By emphasizing Bridget's romantic relationships with Daniel Cleaver and Mark

Darcy, the movie established the love triangle that would repeat frequently in the series.

In this movie, Bridget goes through a process of self-discovery as she comes to accept her flaws and stand up for herself. Her transformation from a lady fixated on social norms to one who embraces herself struck a chord with viewers, positioning her as a representation of strength and fortitude.

Bridget's love mishaps were carried on in the second movie, Bridget Jones: The Edge of Reason, which concentrated on her relationship with Mark Darcy and Daniel Cleaver's comeback. The movie went further into Bridget's fears and the difficulties of sustaining a relationship, even as it preserved the wit and charm of the first installment.

In this movie, Bridget's development is characterized by her increasing self-awareness and will to stand up for her rights. As she learns to negotiate the difficulties of love and trust, her path from self-doubt to self-assurance is a major topic.

To keep Bridget likable and approachable, the movie explored her strengths and weaknesses, giving her more nuance.

Bridget Jones's path underwent a dramatic change in the third movie, Bridget Jones's Baby, as she dealt with the difficulties of pregnancy and parenting. Bridget's character gained significant depth as a result of the movie's emphasis on her work, relationships, and upcoming baby, which reflected the shifting realities and expectations of women in their 40s.

Bridget's perseverance and adaptability are key characteristics of her development in this movie. Her development as a character was demonstrated by her capacity to handle the challenges of pregnancy and the intricacies of her relationships with Mark Darcy and Jack Qwant. To keep Bridget's story current and captivating, the movie's examination of her journey as a soon-to-be mother provides emotional depth.

The most notable development in Bridget's journey is represented by the fourth movie, in which she deals with the difficulties of widowhood, single parenthood, and contemporary dating. Bridget's character is given more depth by the movie's emphasis on her resiliency and self-discovery, which reflects the difficulties of middle age.

Bridget's growth in this movie is characterized by her capacity to face her loss and welcome fresh starts. Her transformation from a distraught widow to a strong and resilient single mother is evidence of her fortitude and tenacity. To keep Bridget's story moving and accessible, the movie delves deeply into her connections with her kids, friends, and new romantic partners.

Her development is marked by themes of empowerment, resiliency, and self-discovery throughout the four films. From her early years as a singleton to her experiences as a mother and widow, each movie focuses on a different stage of her life. The story's decisions—from emphasizing romantic relationships to examining bereavement and single parenthood—reflect the shifting social norms and expectations for women.

Bridget is a timeless and adored figure because of her capacity to handle life's obstacles with elegance, humor, and tenacity. Her development throughout the four movies is evidence of the timeless attraction of her narrative, guaranteeing that she will always be a representation of strength and fortitude.

Comparing the Source Novel

Based on Helen Fielding's 2013 book of the same name, Bridget Jones: Mad About the Boy follows Bridget's journey as a bereaved single mother adjusting to modern life. The movie includes several modifications and adaptations to fit the cinematic medium, while yet staying true to the novel's essence. With an emphasis on the narrative decisions and thematic components that distinguish each, this chapter examines the parallels and discrepancies between the movie and the original book.

The movie captures Bridget's journey through sorrow, single parenthood, and contemporary dating while staying true to the novel's central themes and emotional tone. Both the novel and the movie revolve around Bridget's portrayal as a widowed single mother, her relationships with her kids, and her return to dating. Both pieces are distinguished by their exploration of these subjects through humor and melancholy, which guarantees that the movie keeps the spirit of the book.

The movie includes several modifications and adaptations to fit the cinematic medium, while yet staying true to the novel's concepts. The way Mark Darcy's death is portrayed is among the biggest shifts. Bridget's grieving process is framed by the early revelation of Mark's death in the book. Mark's passing is treated more delicately in the movie, as recollections and flashbacks serve as a moving reminder of his influence on Bridget's life.

To improve the story, the movie also adds new characters and subplots. An important contribution to the movie is the portrayal of Scott Wallaker, a science instructor and single father who serves as Bridget's sympathetic and realistic opposite. The movie develops the subplot about Roxster, a younger man Bridget meets on Tinder, which gives the examination of contemporary dating more depth and fun.

Both the book and the movie depict the intricacies of Bridget's journey by delving into themes of loss, resiliency, and fresh starts. Both pieces emphasize the value of support networks and communities by depicting Bridget's interactions with her kids, friends, and new romantic interests. Both the book and the movie are notable for their exploration of these subjects through humor and sadness, which maintains the emotional impact.

While making adjustments and modifications to fit the cinematic medium, the movie's adaptation of Mad About the Boy stays true to the essence of the book. Both pieces focus on depicting Bridget's experience of sorrow, single parenthood, and contemporary dating, effectively conveying the intricacies and emotional range of her narrative. The film's ability to strike a balance between humor and sorrow guarantees that it will continue to be a respectable adaptation of the original work, appealing to both viewers and novel enthusiasts.

The Movie's Position in the Contemporary Romantic Comedy Genre

By fusing classic components with modern issues and narrative choices, Bridget Jones: Mad About the Boy marks a noteworthy progression in the romantic comedy genre. The film stays current and captivating by examining mourning, single parenthood, and contemporary dating in a way that mirrors audiences' shifting expectations and realities.

From the emphasis on love entanglements to the use of humor and pathos, the movie maintains the classic characteristics of the romantic comedy genre. The story's romantic tension and humorous moments are derived from the depiction of Bridget's interactions with Daniel Cleaver, Scott Wallaker, and Roxster. The romantic comedy genre is known for its ability to strike a balance between humor and emotional depth, which keeps the movie interesting and captivating.

The film differs from conventional romantic comedies in that it explores modern issues including mourning, single parenthood, and modern dating. The film stays contemporary and realistic by reflecting the shifting expectations and realities of viewers through Bridget's portrayal as a bereaved single mother navigating the difficulties of middle age. The usage of dating apps and the examination of age-gap relationships give the story a contemporary feel while illustrating the difficulties of relationships and love in the digital age.

The film's narrative decisions, which range from emphasizing Bridget's grieving process to examining her connections with her kids and new romantic interests, demonstrate how the romantic comedy genre is changing. The genre's flexibility and development are demonstrated by the way Bridget is portrayed as a strong, independent woman who handles life's obstacles with elegance and humor.

Chapter nine

Key Scenes Analysis

One of the most important scenes in Bridget Jones: Mad About the Boy is the memorial service sequence, which captures the unvarnished and complex nature of grief. This chapter explores the memorial service's significance, looking at how it embodies both the larger themes of mourning and resiliency as well as Bridget's experience of loss.

The purpose of the memorial event is to honor Bridget's late husband, Mark Darcy, who was killed while on a humanitarian assignment in Sudan. Friends and family are gathering to pay their respects in a large, solemn location. The mood, which reflects the complexity of mourning, is a blend of celebration and sadness. The service honors Mark's legacy and emphasizes the influence he had on everyone around him, in addition to being a time of sadness.

The memorial service had great emotional value for Bridget. From her first astonishment and incredulity to her eventual acceptance of her new reality, the scenario depicts her effort to manage the intense emotions of loss. The sequence is given depth by the incorporation of flashbacks and recollections of Mark, which serve as a moving reminder of their shared love. Bridget's conversations with friends and family, who give their condolences and support, are intermingled with these moments.

Additionally, the memorial ceremony marks a turning moment in Bridget's life as she starts to face her loss and take the initial steps toward recovery. Renée Zellweger's portrayal, which encapsulates the subtleties of Bridget's journey through bereavement, heightens the scene's emotional impact. The scenario gains depth from her ability to portray both strength and sensitivity, which makes it a potent depiction of loss.

The memorial service scene emphasizes the value of community and support networks in coping with loss, underscoring the film's themes of grief and resiliency. Friends and relatives attending the service give Bridget a sense of comfort and connection by reminding her that she is not traveling alone. From Bridget's private introspection to others' more outward displays of mourning, the scene also examines the various ways people deal with loss.

The film's ability to strike a balance between humor and emotional depth is demonstrated by the scene's use of humor, especially Daniel Cleaver's eulogy. The Bridget Jones series is known for striking this balance, which keeps the depiction of loss realistic and approachable.

Billy's Academic Achievement and Emotional Handling

Billy's performance at school is a pivotal scene that marks a shift in the film's poignant plot.

This chapter examines the performance's relevance, looking at how it depicts Bridget's grieving process as well as the more general themes of healing, family, and resiliency.

An important turning point in the movie is the school performance, which serves as a point of emotional closure for Bridget and her son Billy. The concert honors Billy's late father, Mark Darcy, and is held at his school. Despite his initial hesitancy, Billy's choice to take part in the performance is a turning point in his grieving process and demonstrates his increasing capacity to face and manage his feelings.

The school performance holds great emotional value for Bridget. The scene highlights the difficulties of being a single parent by capturing her attempt to comfort Billy while juggling her own emotions. The sequence is given depth by the inclusion of flashbacks and recollections of Mark, which serve as a moving reminder of their love and the effects of his passing on the family.

Billy's performance of "I'd Do Anything" in honor of his father is a profound moment of emotional closure. The song reminds Bridget of Mark's constant presence in her life and has come to represent the Bridget Jones series. Renée Zellweger's portrayal, which encapsulates the subtleties of Bridget's grieving process and her developing fortitude, heightens the scene's emotional impact.

The film's themes of family and resiliency are emphasized in the school performance sequence, which also emphasizes how crucial support and connection are when dealing with loss. Attending the show with friends and family gives Bridget and Billy a sense of comfort and connection by reminding them that they are not traveling alone. The scenario also examines the various ways that people deal with loss, from Bridget's steadfast support to Billy's quiet resolve.

The film's ability to strike a balance between humor and emotional depth is demonstrated by the scene's use of humor, especially in the interactions between Bridget and her friends.

The Bridget Jones series is known for striking this balance, which keeps the depiction of loss realistic and approachable.

Scene from the Last Party: Significance and Settlement

The last party scene is a joyous and symbolic occasion that signifies the end of Bridget's grieving process and her acceptance of fresh starts. This chapter examines the meaning of the movie's climactic party scene and how it embodies its themes of resiliency, camaraderie, and the potential for happiness.

On New Year's Eve, Bridget and her loved ones are gathering to commemorate the start of a new year in the last party scene. With bright decorations, upbeat music, and an air of happiness and hope, the scene is set in a lively and celebratory setting. The mood, which combines joy and introspection, perfectly captures the film's themes of resiliency and fresh starts.

The last party scene holds great emotional significance for Bridget. Her mourning journey and her developing capacity to seize new opportunities are depicted in the scene. The setting is given a sense of hope and promise by the presence of Scott Wallaker, with whom she has developed a close bond. Bridget's relationships with her friends and family serve as a reminder of the value of support and community in overcoming obstacles in life.

As Bridget considers her trip and the lessons she has learned, the last party scene also acts as a moment of emotional closure. The sequence is given depth by the inclusion of flashbacks and recollections of Mark, which serve as a moving reminder of their love and the effects of his passing on her life. Renée Zellweger's portrayal, which encapsulates the subtleties of Bridget's grieving process and her developing fortitude, heightens the scene's emotional impact.

The film's themes of resiliency and fresh starts are emphasized in the film's last party scene, which also emphasizes how crucial support and connection are while overcoming obstacles in life. The party's attendance of friends and relatives gives Bridget a sense of security and camaraderie by serving as a reminder that she is not traveling alone. From Bridget's private introspection to the more outward displays of happiness and celebration, the scene also examines the many ways people deal with loss.

An intense moment of emotional closure occurs at the end of the sequence when Bridget and Scott share a kiss as the clock strikes midnight. The kiss represents Bridget's capacity to welcome fresh chances and discover joy despite the loss. The scene's use of color and light evokes a feeling of coziness and hope, which supports the film's theme of fortitude and optimism.

Chapter ten

Fan Experience and Community

Audiences' responses to the 2025 release of Bridget Jones: Mad About the Boy ranged widely, from passionate acclaim to heated discussions on the film's narrative decisions. Both new and seasoned series fans expressed their opinions, views, and feelings on forums, fan communities, and social media. The various audience responses and fan theories that surfaced following the premiere of the movie are examined in this chapter.

The film's emotional resonance was one of the most often expressed reactions. With special attention to Renée Zellweger's portrayal of Bridget, many viewers commended the film for its empathetic depiction of sorrow, single parenthood, and contemporary dating. Fans said that it felt like a logical development for the character and praised the movie's ability to strike a balance between humor and emotional depth. Viewers who could identify with Bridget's journey shared their tales of loss, resiliency, and fresh starts on social media in droves.

The choice to eliminate Colin Firth's character, Mark Darcy, was one of the most contentious elements of the movie. Some fans were disappointed by the passing of a cherished character, while others praised the daring creative decision that gave Bridget's journey more emotional weight. Discussions concerning whether Mark's death was essential to the plot were common in online forums and fan communities, with some fans speculating about possible storylines that would have kept him alive.

Fan theories were triggered by the film's unresolved ending, which depicts Bridget falling in love with Scott Wallaker while paying tribute to Mark. A fifth movie that would examine Bridget's relationship with Scott and her ongoing journey as a single mother was the subject of some fan speculation. Others speculated about Hugh Grant's character Daniel Cleaver's possible comeback and his changing significance in Bridget's life. Talks concerning Roxster and Scott's potential future roles in the franchise also arose from the introduction of new characters.

Audiences responded favorably to the film's examination of modern issues like age-gap relationships, modern dating, and single parenthood, which sparked more extensive cultural discussions. The film's relevant and relatable depiction of these concerns won plaudits from fans, who pointed out that it mirrored the shifting expectations and reality of contemporary life. The movie's ability to strike a balance between classic romantic comedy components and modern concerns made sure that both new viewers and devoted viewers found it interesting and relevant.

Marketing, Social Media, and Merchandise Campaigns

A thorough marketing strategy that used merchandising, social media, and strategic alliances to create awareness and engage viewers was launched alongside the release of Bridget Jones: Mad About the Boy. This chapter looks at the movie's marketing tactics and how they affected its box office performance.

To keep fans interested and create anticipation for the release, the movie's merchandising was crucial. The merchandising leveraged the franchise's nostalgic appeal while adding fresh components that mirrored the film's themes, from Bridget's recognizable diary-inspired notebooks to apparel lines with passages from the movie. Fans were especially drawn to limited-edition products, which evoked a feeling of exclusivity and expectation. These included signed posters and collectible figurines.

The marketing strategy for the movie was created to appeal to both new and devoted viewers. Renée Zellweger's comeback as Bridget and the debut of new characters were highlighted in trailers and advertising materials, which also highlighted the film's humor and emotional depth. With partnerships and themed marketing that tapped into the love themes, the campaign also took advantage of the Valentine's Day release of the movie.

With a focused campaign that engaged fans and created buzz, social media was a key component of the movie's marketing plan. Behind-the-scenes photos, exclusive videos, and interactive updates that promoted fan interaction were shared via the movie's official accounts on social media sites like Facebook, Instagram, and Twitter. Fans felt excited and connected as a result of hashtags like MadAboutTheBoy and BridgetJones2025 trending on social media.

Influencers and celebrities who expressed their enthusiasm for the movie and urged their followers to see it were also included in the marketing. Through these collaborations, the movie was able to reach a wider audience and appeal to younger viewers, keeping it current in the digital era.

A major contributor to the movie's financial success was its marketing strategy, which created excitement and expectation that resulted in a successful box office run and high streaming figures. The film's ongoing appeal was aided by the campaign's ability to strike a balance between nostalgia and innovation, which made it appealing to both new and devoted viewers.

The Development of Bridget Jones Fan Communities

An important turning point in the development of Bridget Jones fan networks was the publication of Bridget Jones: Mad About the Boy. The premiere of the movie generated a new level of enthusiasm and involvement among fans, as seen by everything from fan conventions and events to online forums and social media organizations. The development of Bridget Jones fan communities and their influence on the movie's cultural impact are examined in this chapter.

The cultural effect of the Bridget Jones franchise has always included active and thriving fan networks. Fans were able to express their opinions, hypotheses, and feelings about the movie on online forums and social media communities including Facebook groups and Reddit threads. Fans speculated about the narrative, shared their favorite scenes from the previous movies, and talked about their expectations for Mad About the Boy in these forums, which were especially busy in the run-up to the movie's release.

The premiere of the movie caused a flurry of activity in these communities, with fans debating the film's narrative decisions in great detail, making fan art, and discussing their views. Discussions concerning their roles in the franchise and possible influence on the next movies were sparked by the arrival of new characters like Roxster and Scott Wallaker.

Fan conventions and activities devoted to the Bridget Jones franchise also saw a rebirth following the publication of Mad About the Boy. These gatherings gave fans a chance to interact with the cast and crew, celebrate their passion for the show, and unite. Popular elements of these gatherings were panels, Q&A sessions, and showings of the earlier movies, which helped fans feel connected and part of a community.

The film's examination of modern issues, such as single parenthood and modern dating, also sparked conversations and workshops at these gatherings, demonstrating the franchise's capacity to strike a deep and intimate chord with viewers.

From influencing marketing tactics to offering input on the movies, Bridget Jones fan communities have been crucial in forming the franchise's cultural effect. With every new release igniting a fresh feeling of excitement and engagement, the brand has managed to stay relevant and captivating because of the passion and dedication of these communities.

An important turning point in the development of these communities was the publication of Mad About the Boy, which demonstrated the franchise's flexibility in responding to the times. The film's examination of modern issues and skill at striking a balance between humor and emotional depth made it appealing to both new and returning viewers, adding to the Bridget Jones series' ongoing popularity.

Made in the USA
Middletown, DE
22 April 2025

74637253R00057